WARREN HAYNES
Guide to Slide Guitar

Recording credits:

Warren Haynes, *slide guitar*

Matt Abts, *drums*

Danny Lewis, *keyboards*

Andy Hess, *bass*

Mike Levine, *rhythm guitar*
(tracks 48 and 49), *producer and audio editor*

Michael Barbiero, *engineer*

Produced by Warren Haynes with Mike Levine

Cover photos and photo on page 4 by Brian Shupe
Photo on page 7 by Mike Levine

ISBN 978-1-57560-524-1

7777 W. BLUEMOUND RD. P.O. BOX 13819 MILWAUKEE, WI 53213

Visit Hal Leonard Online at
www.halleonard.com

PLAYBACK+
Speed • Pitch • Balance • Loop

To access audio visit:
www.halleonard.com/mylibrary

Enter Code
7041-3636-3305-6368

TABLE OF CONTENTS

INTRODUCTION

1

Welcome to *The Warren Haynes Guide to Slide Guitar*. Here, I explain my method for playing slide, and even provide you with recorded examples of the major concepts. I suggest that you go through each of the examples (presented here in both standard notation and tablature) slowly and deliberately, learning the licks and solos by playing along. By doing so, you'll get insights into my approach to slide. You can then incorporate that approach into your playing and develop your own unique style.

There are two different types of audio examples: those with rhythm section backup and solo tracks. On the latter, you can hear the slide through both the left and right speakers. On the examples with a rhythm section (which are the majority), the slide is panned all the way to the left, and the rhythm section all the way to the right. This enables you to isolate the slide part when you're trying to hear a subtle nuance, or turn it off completely so you can play along with the rhythm section. For your convenience, the rhythm section tracks for five of the full-length solos, including an extended version of the "Jazzy Solo," are repeated on tracks 50–54.

Warren Haynes

Learn all you can from the book—but most of all, have fun!

Warren Haynes

ABOUT THE AUTHORS

Warren Haynes is recognized as one of the leading slide guitarists of his time. He's a founding member and frontman of Gov't Mule and is a regular member of the Allman Brothers Band and Phil Lesh and Friends. Haynes has recorded numerous CDs, playing both slide and standard guitar, and has appeared on CDs for many other artists. Originally from Asheville, North Carolina, Haynes now lives in the New York City area.

Mike Levine is a musician, author, and editor. This is his fifth book (four for Cherry Lane and one for *Billboard* Books). He is also a senior editor at *Electronic Musician* magazine. Levine plays guitar, dobro, and pedal steel, has played in numerous bands and on Broadway (*The Will Rogers Follies*), and has composed music for television. Visit his website at www.mikelevine.com.

CHAPTER I

GETTING STARTED

STANDARD VS. OPEN TUNING

Before I explain my slide style and approach, I'll talk briefly about tuning.

Although many slide players use open tunings, I prefer, for the most part, to play in standard tuning. I've been able to develop a style in which I can emulate various open tunings while keeping all of the advantages of playing in standard tuning.

What are those advantages? For one thing, I have all of the notes and scales available to me that I'm used to from regular, non-slide playing; this makes it much easier for me to play against non-standard changes, minor chords, and so forth. In addition, playing in standard tuning allows me to easily switch over to non-slide parts (both lead and rhythm) in the middle of a song without having to change guitars.

Since this book is meant to reflect my style of slide playing, all of the examples are in standard tuning. So tune it up just like you always do, and let's get started!

SLIDE TYPES

I prefer to use a glass slide—in particular, an old Coricidin bottle, which is what Duane Allman used. Although Coricidin doesn't come in glass bottles anymore, you can find reissues out there that are made very well. The only problem with playing slide with a Coricidin bottle is that, because it's closed at one end, moisture tends to build up in it.

I also have ceramic and brass slides, and I have the normal steel ones, too, but glass seems to work best for me. However, it's totally a matter of taste, so experiment with different types and use what you like best.

FINGER CHOICES

I wear my slide on my ring finger but, again, it's really a matter of choice. Duane Allman wore his on his ring finger, but Lowell George used his pinkie. Bonnie Raitt and Jeff Beck put their slides on their middle fingers. Of course, if you're going to play rhythm and non-slide lead while wearing a slide, you'll need to take that into consideration. I recommend that you make your decision based not only on what's comfortable for you for slide playing, but what's easiest for playing chords.

PICKS VS. FINGERS

Like many slide players, I mainly pluck the strings of the guitar with my fingers instead of a flatpick. I find that this gives me much greater control and makes it possible for me to *dampen* strings with my right hand (more about that in a moment), which makes for a much cleaner tone. That said, there are times when I want the extra intensity and sharper attack that a pick brings, so I sometimes do use one.

To show you the difference in tone, here's the same lick played twice: the first time with fingers and the second time with a pick. Notice that the second example sounds brighter, but also has more overtones because I can't dampen with my right hand if I'm holding a pick.

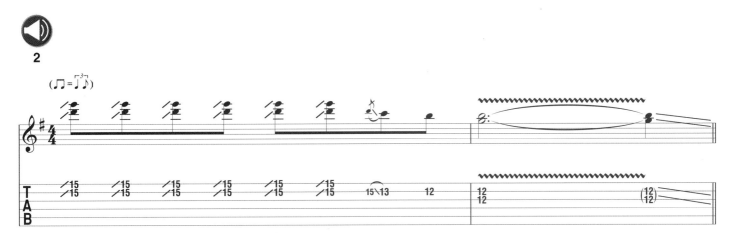

DAMPENING

Dampening involves muting strings to cut down on the overtones and noises that occur when you move a slide on the steel strings of a guitar.

You can dampen with both your left hand (slide hand) and your right hand (pick hand), but the latter is the more important. I use the fingers that I'm not plucking with to mute the strings that I don't want to sound. For instance, when I'm plucking a string with my index finger, I use my middle finger on one side and my thumb on the other side to mute out the surrounding strings. In addition, I also use the side of my palm for additional muting. Dampening takes some getting used to; when I first started playing I had to think about it all the time, but now it's second nature. It's a crucial skill to master if you're going to become a proficient slide player.

This photo shows my right-hand dampening technique. I've just plucked the B string with my index finger and am dampening the surrounding strings—the G string with my thumb and the E string with my middle finger.

You can also dampen with your left hand by resting your fingers on the strings behind the slide. By dampening with both your left and right hands, you'll find that you can get a much cleaner sound.

Dampening is particularly important when playing slide in standard tuning. In open tunings, there are always chord tones under your slide (assuming that you have your slide at the correct fret), but in standard tuning, only some of the notes at a given fret will be correct, and you'll have to dampen out the others.

This is an example of a melodic, Delta-style slide lick. As in most cases, I dampen with both my left and right hands.

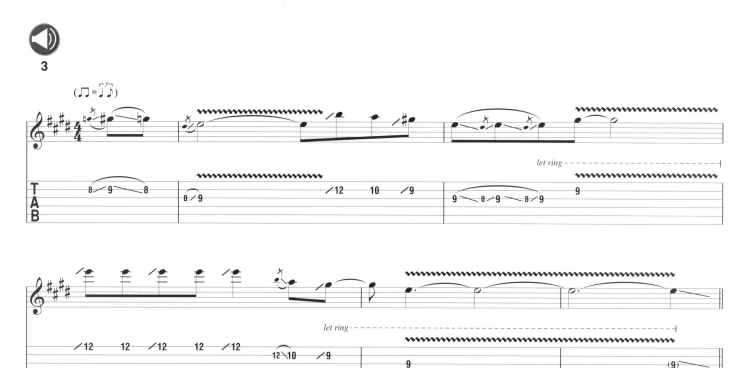

To show you how important it is to dampen, I play this next riff without any dampening at all. Notice all of the overtones and unwanted notes that get in. This should demonstrate to you why it's crucial to master the art of dampening.

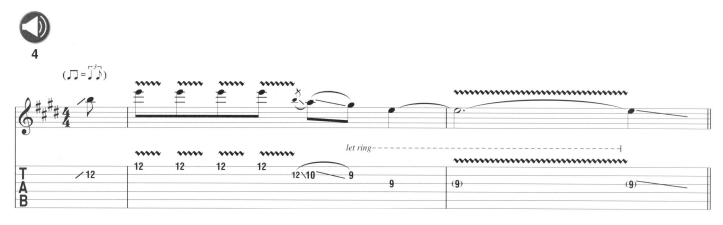

For effect, I sometimes lift up my index and middle fingers on my left hand behind the slide so that the only dampening is coming from my right hand. Doing so creates a raspy, more Delta-like sound (as in this example), as opposed to the more concise, cleaner sound that comes from dampening with both hands. It all depends on what type of sound you're going for.

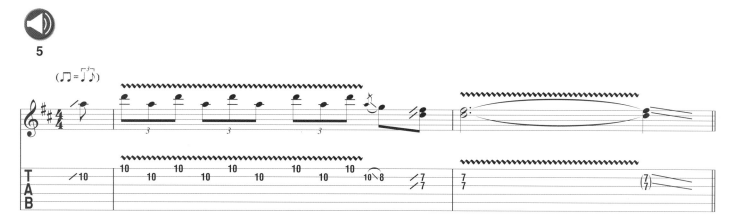

SLIDE PLACEMENT

One problem that some players have when learning slide is bad intonation. Unlike non-slide guitar, where you place your left-hand fingers in between the frets, slide requires that you place the center of your slide directly over the fret. It's a little bit of an adjustment from standard fretting, but you can get used to it pretty quickly.

When you play on the open E string (or any open string, for that matter) and then go up to the 12th fret, you want to make sure that those two notes are in tune with each other. Here is a good exercise for your ear—it will help with the intonation of your slide playing.

6

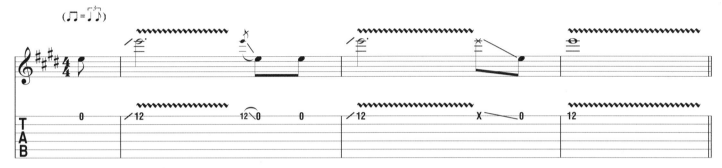

VIBRATO

Vibrato is very important in playing slide. Not only does it add expression to your playing, but it helps with your intonation. This is because the slide moves back and forth while you apply vibrato—this "fudges" the pitch of the note, making it sound more in tune.

The greater the distance (horizontally) that you move the slide back and forth, the more pronounced the vibrato effect will be, and the more it will affect the pitch of the note. The faster you move the slide, the more intense the vibrato effect will be.

I use several types of vibrato. Most of the time I use a slow, not too wide, somewhat subtle vibrato. Other times, I use a wider, faster vibrato for a more pronounced effect. Let's look at a couple of examples.

Here, I use a slow (or light) vibrato. For that long, held note that goes over the last two measures, I start the note without any vibrato, and then add it later as the note sustains. This mimics what singers often do when they start running out of breath—this helps them to sustain a note.

7

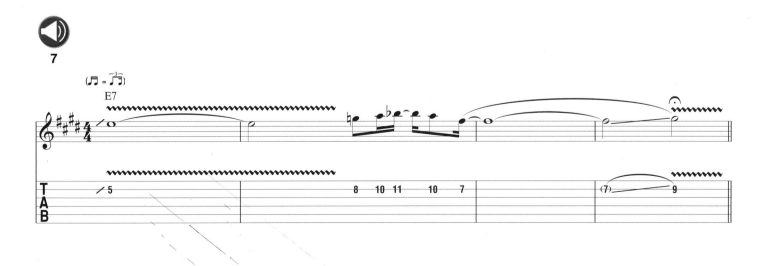

In this example, I use a much quicker, angrier vibrato, which gives the sound a more intense, Elmore James–type feel.

8

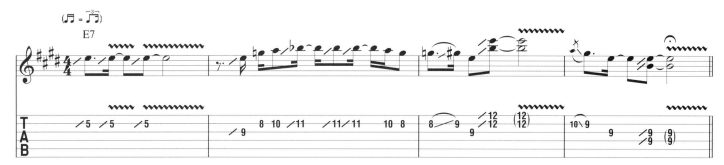

PLAYING RHYTHM

One of the many advantages of playing slide in standard tuning is that you can easily play rhythm guitar parts when called upon, without having to switch guitars or retune. The only real impediment you have to rhythm playing is the slide itself—sometimes you'll have time to take it off to play rhythm, but often you won't. This means that it's important to learn to play rhythm parts with the slide on your finger. If you wear it on your ring finger, like I do, it can take some getting used to (rhythm playing is easier if you wear the slide on your pinkie).

Here are a couple of Choruses of a blues progression in which I'm playing various rhythm parts while wearing the slide. Although the parts may not seem difficult by themselves, try practicing them with your slide on. It may take some getting used to.

9

CHAPTER 2

APPROACHING THE NECK

Because I play slide in standard tuning, it makes it much easier for me to envision the neck and know where I can and cannot play. Because I dampen the strings when I play, I can use the slide virtually anywhere on the neck, just as when I'm playing regular guitar parts.

In order to mimic the sound of open tuning, however, you need to find chords that you can play *with the slide*. Open tuning has the potential for six chord tones on each fret, but the best you can do in standard tuning is to find three on a fret—on the 2nd, 3rd, and 4th strings, creating a *triad*, or three-note chord. There are also several places on the neck to find two-note chords, or *dyads*. You can use these triads and dyads as center points for your slide playing.

In this example, I center my playing on triads found on the 7th fret (I chord), 12th fret (IV chord), and 14th fret (V chord). When you play slide in standard tuning, you find yourself centered on the "triad position" quite a bit.

10

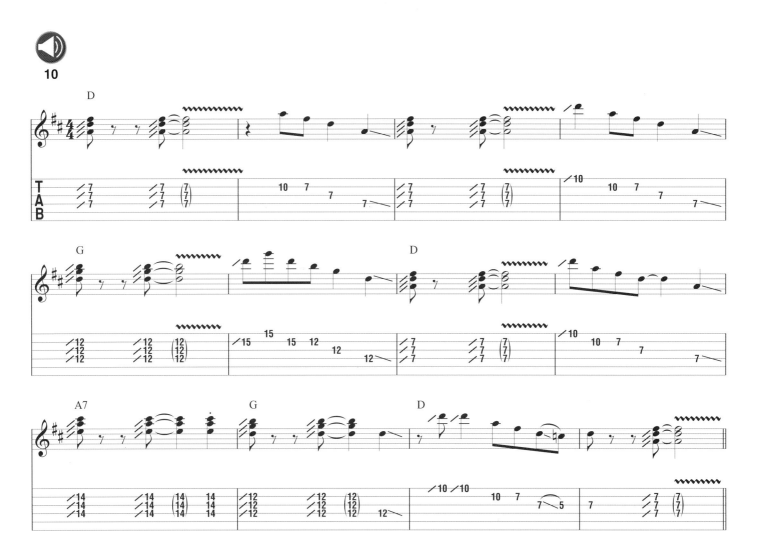

In this example, I center my playing around a dyad on the E and B strings throughout most of the progression. I mix in a couple of dyads from the G and D strings (measures 9 and 10), which are actually in the same positions as the triads in the last example, but without the 3rds added.

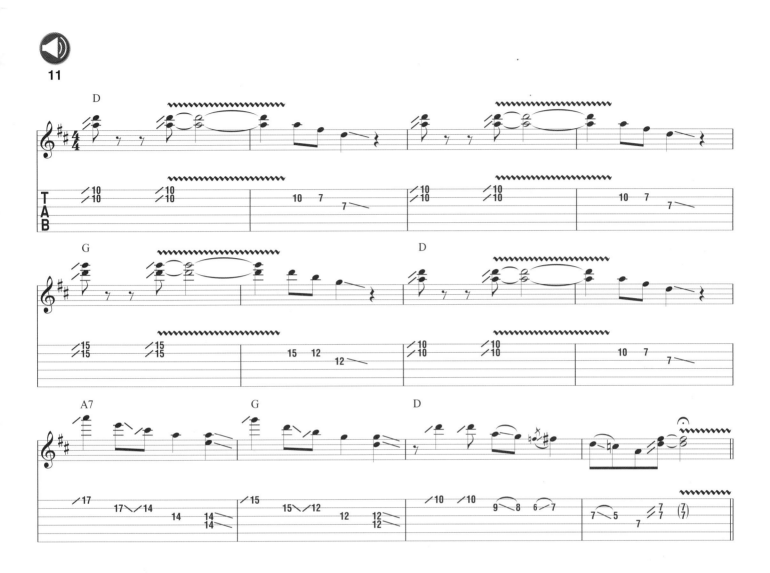

Although you can find the same notes in several places on the neck, the sound you get varies depending on which strings you use for a given lick.

It's important to learn all of the notes on the fretboard so you'll know all of the places you can find the same notes (and play the same licks). For one thing, this allows you to play a given lick without having to stretch too far. It also lets you choose the actual sound you're going for. For instance, when you play a lick on fatter strings, you get a fatter sound.

Here's a diagram to get you started—it shows the E chord triads and dyads available in standard tuning.

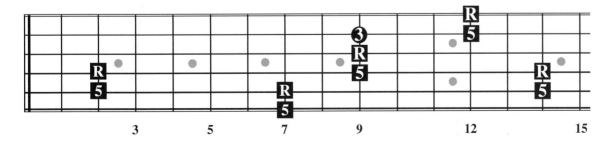

This next example involves playing the same lick in three different positions on the neck. The same lick might be played very differently by different players, depending on the sound they're going for. A lick that Ry Cooder might play on the higher strings to get that "Ry Cooder sound," Duane Allman might have chosen to play on the lower strings (albeit in the same register) to get that thicker, "Duane Allman sound." Sometimes it's not the sound that dictates where you choose to play a particular lick, but more a matter of its proximity to the last lick you played—in other words, it's easy to get to.

MIMICKING OPEN E

Despite the advantages that I mentioned earlier, playing slide in standard tuning requires more effort (at least at the beginning) when you're trying to emulate the sound of open tunings. Many characteristic slide licks were developed in open tunings (mostly open E and open G) and just "lay" better in those tunings. Open E is one of the most popular—Duane Allman used it, and Derek Trucks uses it—and much of the slide repertoire is in that tuning.

To get that open E sound in standard tuning, you have to work a little harder at first. You have to move the slide around a bit more in many situations, but once you get used to this, you'll actually have more melodic freedom and flexibility than in an open tuning.

To give you an idea, the following are some open E–style licks arranged for standard tuning.

Let's start simple with an Elmore James "Dust My Broom"–type lick. In open E, this would all sit nicely on one fret, but in standard tuning, you have to move from the 12th fret—first for the A and G♯ notes, and then again for the E and G♯ on the 9th fret.

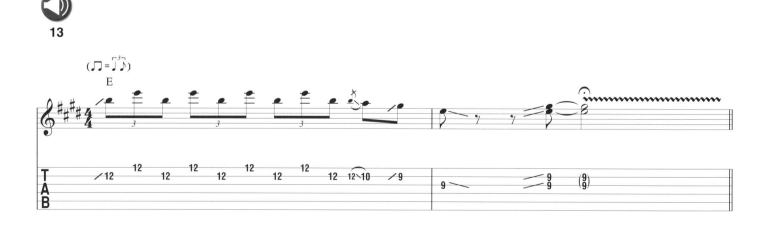

This next one's a little slower and more in the style of Muddy Waters. Here, I use a triad (in this case, an A chord on the 14th fret) as the center position for the lick. Notice how I slide up to the E note each time, giving the lick a greater sense of urgency.

For this open E–type lick in C, pay attention to how I play the 3rd of a C chord (E) on the 9th fret of the G string (second to last measure) and then resolve it to the dyad on the 10th fret of the D and A strings. Picture, if you will, that E note as being in the middle of a C triad (like one you'd play on rhythm guitar) with a G above it on the 2nd string, 8th fret, and a C below it on the 4th string, 10 fret. Grabbing the 3rd of a chord out of that position is something you do quite a bit when you're emulating the style of open tuning in standard tuning.

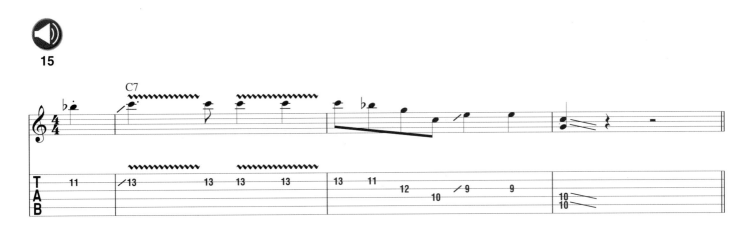

Playing on the low strings makes for a rounder, fatter sound. For this low-down and nasty lick, I use the open 6th string to start it off and do a lot of sliding up into the notes. I end with a dyad on the 5th and 6th strings at the 7th fret.

Here's a Duane Allman–style lick featuring his very characteristic back-and-forth motion. This would sit more comfortably in open E; in standard tuning it requires more concentration and a greater span of movement between the highest and lowest notes. It also requires that you dampen very carefully because you'll get nasty, wrong notes if you let the G string sound while you're playing the B string on the 10th and 8th frets. Once you practice this enough, though, it will start to feel very comfortable.

CHAPTER 3
PLAYING THE BLUES

There are many different types of blues licks that you can play with a slide, giving you a variety of feels. From old fashioned, Delta-style licks to more rock-influenced riffs, there is a wide range of possibilities at your disposal.

I've already shown you a number of examples of playing against the I chord and making it sound like open E tuning. In a moment, I'll cover my approach to the IV and V chords—but first, here are a few more examples of playing against the I chord. (Note that you could move these licks up a 4th or a 5th and use them against a IV or V chord, respectively, if you wanted to.)

This Delta-style passage in E utilizes the open 1st and 2nd strings and ends with a big slide up to a dyad on the 12th fret. Notice how I bounce the slide a little on the C# note in the pickup, creating almost a hammer-on effect. Also note the use of both minor and major 3rds, helping to create that Delta feel.

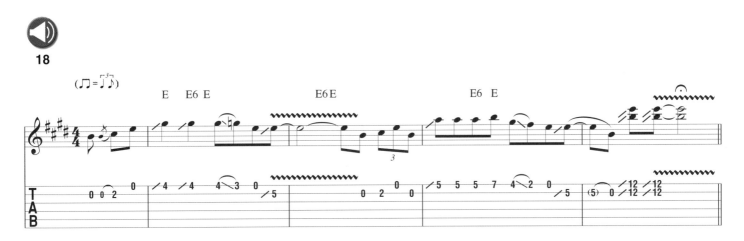

This passage in A is like something Duane Allman would play. It's got that back-and-forth movement in measures 1 and 3, and ends up on an A triad at the 14th fret.

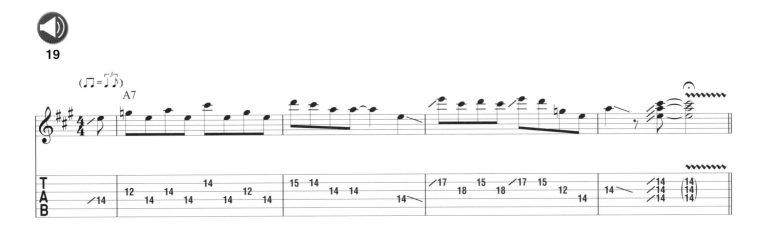

Here, I play against the I chord with a more melodic feel. The C# in the first measure and the G# in the last measure help keep things sounding like they're in E major.

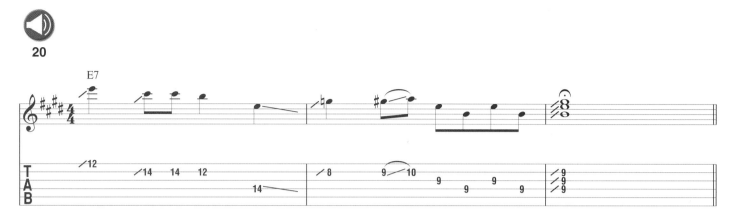

Here's another characteristic slide lick, featuring a large leap (over an octave) to the high E.

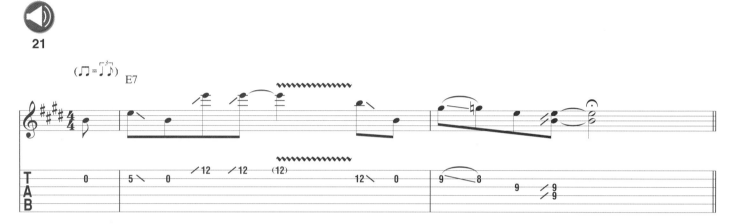

GOING TO IV AND V

There are several ways that I approach going to the IV chord in a blues progression. As stated, you can move your slide up five frets from the position you used playing against the I chord and then play similar licks that are a 4th higher. Or, you can stay where you are and play similar licks without moving to the next chord, which is what I call playing "across" the IV chord (as opposed to playing "inside" the chord when you're going specifically for chord tones). You may have to change a note here or there, and you won't want to play, for example, the G# note of an E chord against an A chord, but most of your licks will work. In a lot of old-time blues, when the band is playing a V chord, the singer or the soloist is still "kind of" playing the I, even though the tonic note is not in the V chord. There's something beautiful about that. You get the best of both worlds if you vary what you do—play inside the chord one minute and outside it the next.

In this example, the tonic note (D) that I play against the I chord is the 5th of the IV chord, so it works just fine in both cases. The one "concession" that I made to the IV is the G that I feature in the third measure.

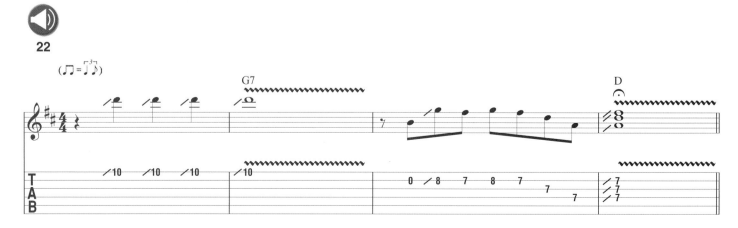

Here's a walk up to the IV chord in C, in which I play more inside the IV chord. I play some notes here (especially the F and the E♭) that are part of the F7 (IV7) chord, but would sound wrong if played against the I. That E♭ in the third measure makes things feel almost minor for a minute, and that's very bluesy. Minor 3rds and flat 7ths can give a line a truly bluesy feel.

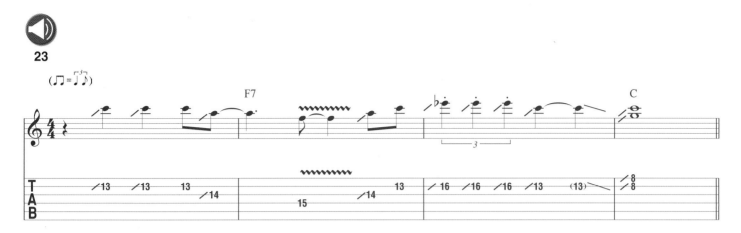

In this example, I chose to play pretty much inside the V chord—most of the notes are from an A triad on the 14th fret. Also notice that I've again employed that back-and-forth type of motion that's so characteristic of the Allman Brothers slide sound.

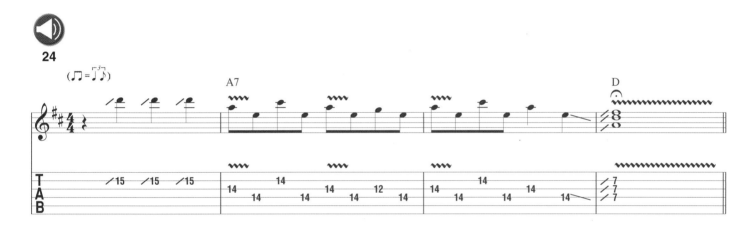

I take a different approach to the V chord here by playing "across" it—essentially ignoring it and playing notes that I would play against the I chord. It's not as melodic-sounding, but it works. The real old-school blues players often treated every chord as the same—the chords underneath would change, but the scales on top would not.

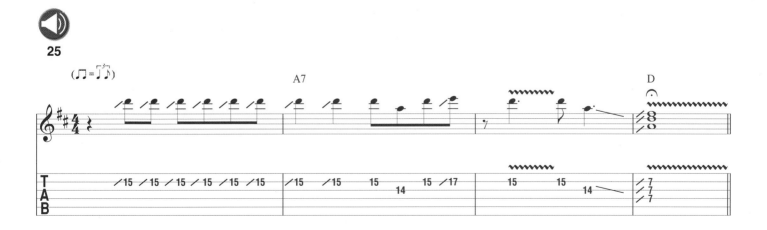

For this V–IV–I progression, I play inside the V chord and then pretty much ignore the IV chord. I sometimes move with the chords when playing blues, and sometimes don't. It's good to mix it up and keep things fresh. There are no rules except that it has to sound good.

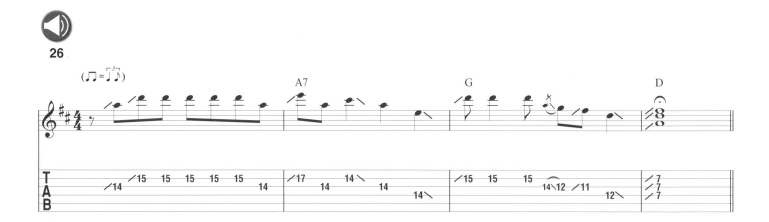

TURNAROUNDS

At the end of a blues progression, the *turnaround* serves as the transition into the next Chorus. Here are examples that show some of what I like to do with turnarounds. The next two examples also show more approaches to V–IV–I.

In the two first full measures leading up to this turnaround, I start in the *E triad position* on the 9th fret (called so because you get an E triad from the notes on the 2nd, 3rd, and 4th strings at that fret), and then use notes from the A minor pentatonic scale (from the 8th to the 10th frets) to get to I in measure 3. The turnaround itself is centered around the tonic, and afterwards I do some syncopated comping until the fadeout.

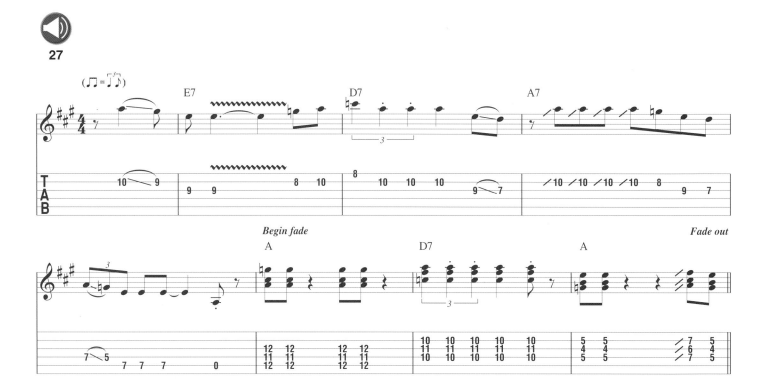

This turnaround is from a slow blues in G. Notice how I leap up to the high G note in measure 3—that jump in register gives the turnaround a kick-start of energy.

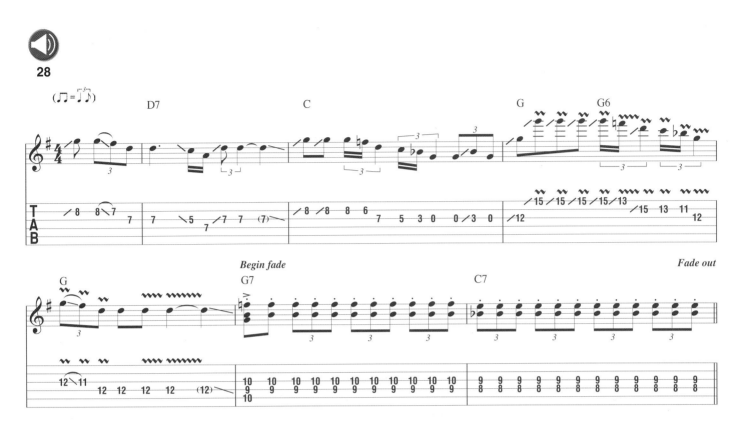

Now that we've looked at the different parts of a blues progression, let's put it all together into a full blues shuffle solo. In the first Chorus of the solo, notice how everything is centered around the G triad on the 12th fret (with the exception of a couple of leaps up to the high C on the E string, 20th fret). I bring the intensity down a little in the beginning of the second Chorus and then build it back up. Notice the use of the open G string in measure 14 and the heavy vibrato in measures 21 and 22.

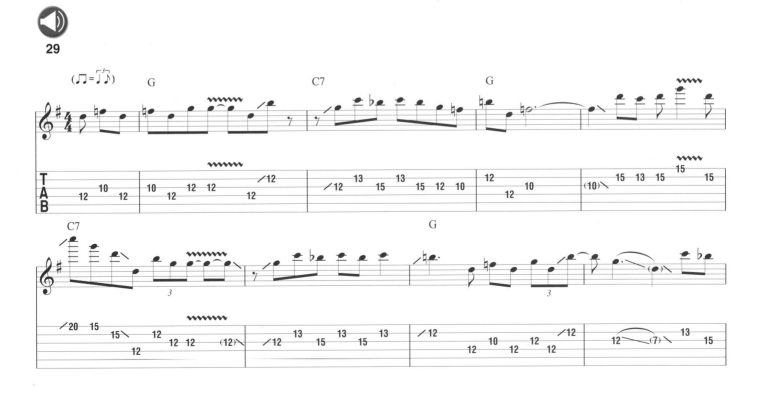

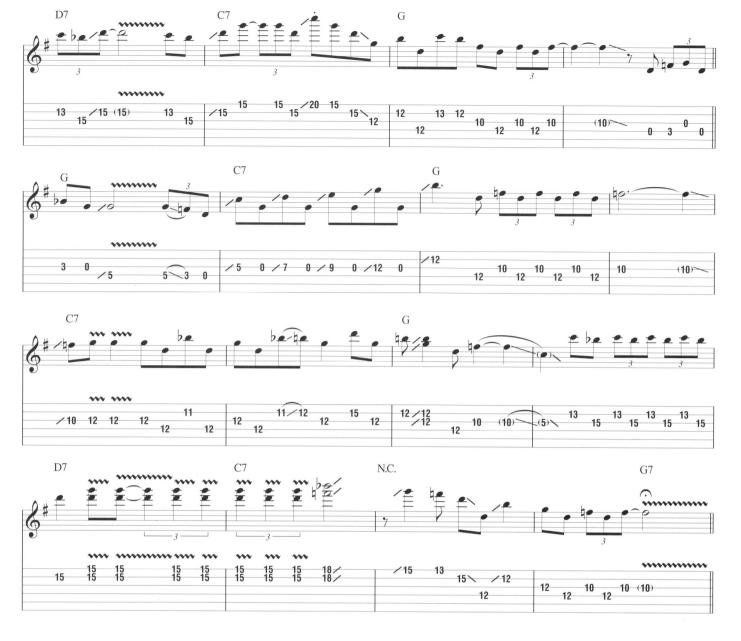

SLOW BLUES

Let's slow it down for the moment, and I'll demonstrate some of my slow blues slide playing. When you play slowly, you have more occasions to use vibrato because you tend to hold notes for longer durations and play more expressively.

This slow blues lick in the key of E sounds a bit like Muddy would have played it. Notice the heavy vibrato on the E at the end of measure 1.

30

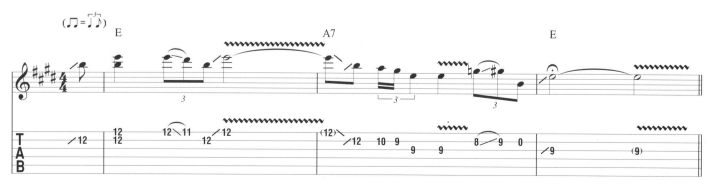

Here's another Muddy Water's–like slow lick in the key of A. I use a lot of vibrato here, both in the beginning and at the end, where you may notice that it helps with intonation.

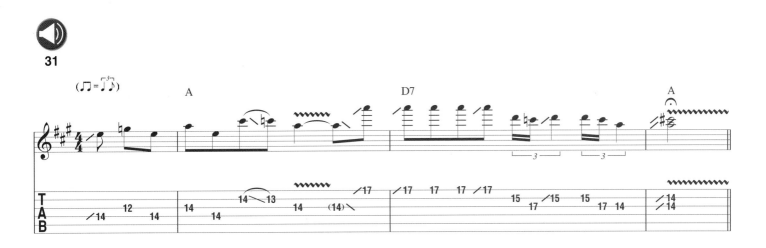

This slow solo includes much of the stuff we've talked about so far: how to ignore chords, how to play inside chords, how to change your note selection (or not) when you're playing against the V. I also vary my approaches to vibrato, attack, and dynamics here, changing up all of the things that make the blues fun.

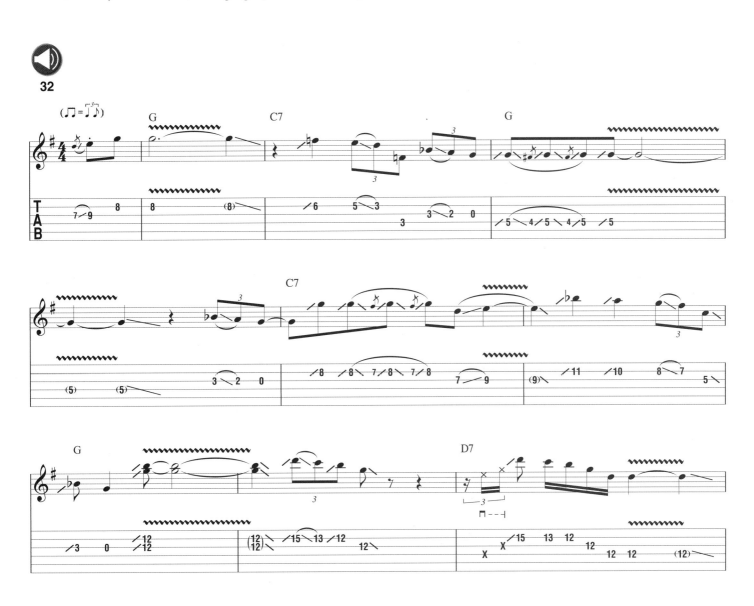

CHAPTER 4
ADVANCED SOLOING

In this section, I'll demonstrate some of the trickier techniques that I use in my playing. You don't want to overuse them, but they do add flash to solos.

One of the techniques I use quite a bit is playing legato, which here means to pluck just once at the beginning of a riff and then move the slide around to produce the other notes as the string continues to vibrate. This technique adds a gospel feel to your playing and emulates a pedal steel or lap steel. Although I do a couple of different legato licks in this example, the most characteristic one occurs at the end of the first full measure.

33

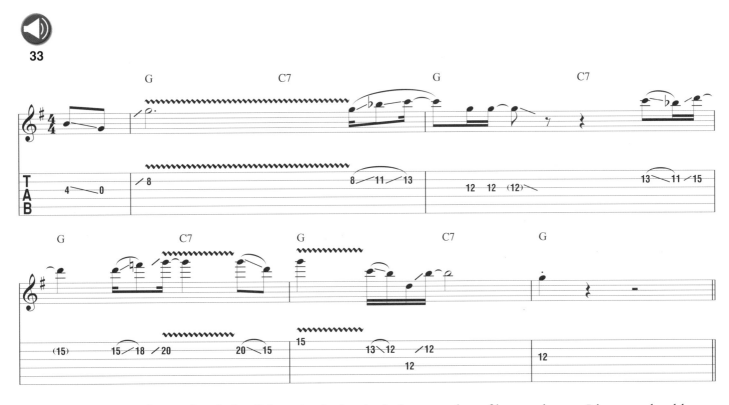

Here's another gospel-tinged melodic slide example that includes a number of legato phrases. It's somewhat bluesy, but more melodic than what I'd play against a standard blues progression.

34

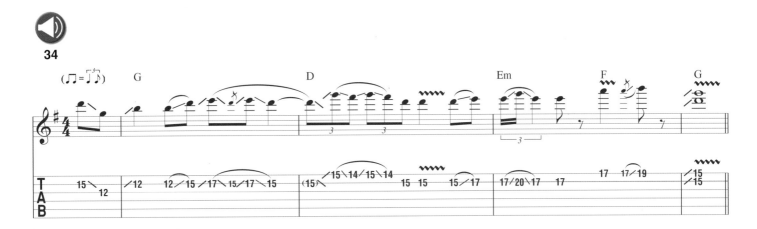

Another advanced technique is to play really high up on the neck—in this case, actually above the fretboard. On most guitars, you have to pivot your slide hand in order to fret a note correctly up there. I'm playing that high E octave with a wide, intense vibrato.

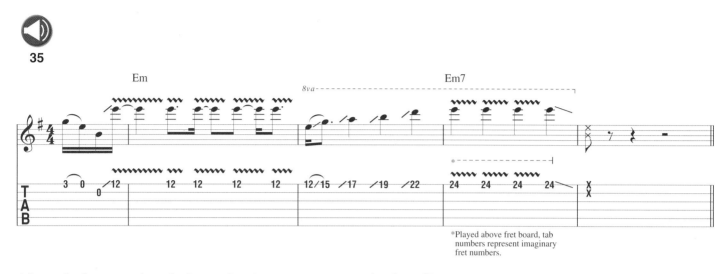

This solo features a lot of advanced techniques. For example, the riff in measure 19 (starting on the 3rd string, 12th fret) is a pretty tough one to dampen correctly. This is because it moves around from string-to-string and fret-to-fret quite a bit; you have to really concentrate on your dampening or you'll get a lot of extraneous notes. Other things to look for in this solo are the slide "hammer-ons" in measure 21, and the extremely high fretboard work and heavy vibrato in measures 22–24. Work on this solo slowly, a little bit at a time, and you'll end up learning quite a few techniques.

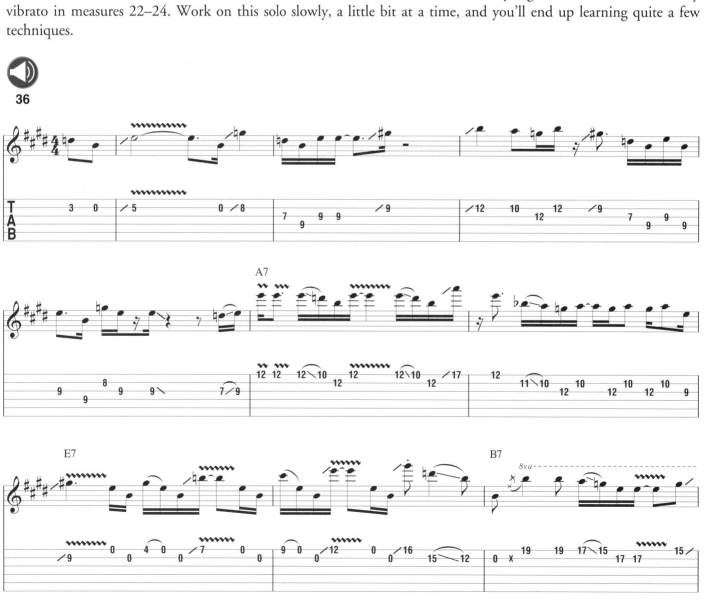

CHAPTER 5

BEYOND THE I–IV–V

One of the advantages of playing in standard tuning is that you don't have to think about transposing—you can play essentially as you do regular guitar, and it's much easier to play against minor chords and tricky chord changes. Why? It's simple: The notes that work when you're playing *without* a slide also work when you're playing *with* a slide. I'll start with some minor key slide examples, and then move on to some examples featuring non-standard changes.

In this example, I start with an Am triad at the 5th fret, and end on the A note on the 4th string, 7th fret. Be particularly careful to dampen the 3rd, 2nd, and 1st strings on the 7th fret when you hit that A—you don't want those notes to sound.

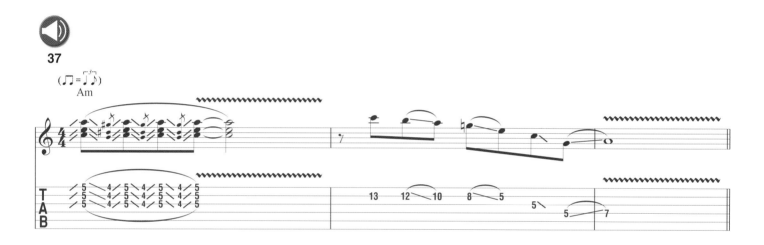

Here's an uptempo example in minor. When you're playing against minor chords in standard tuning (or any tuning, for that matter), you should, for the most part, avoid the major 3rd and the major 6th, but it depends on the chord progression.

In this i–iv–i example in Am, I use mostly notes from the A blues scale (A–C–D–E♭–E–G♭, or an Am pentatonic scale with a ♭5). Although there are many ways to attack the iv chord, here I slide up to a D. I avoid major 3rds and major 6ths throughout, although I do hit one major 3rd as a passing tone in the second to last measure.

This solo demonstrates the freedom you have in standard tuning when playing against minor cords—you can play pretty much the same notes as you would if you were playing without a slide. This example also demonstrates the importance of pacing in a solo. Notice how I take a couple of big pauses in the first five measures, kind of like the breaths a horn player might take. Putting such "breaths" in a solo really helps the notes that you do play to stand out.

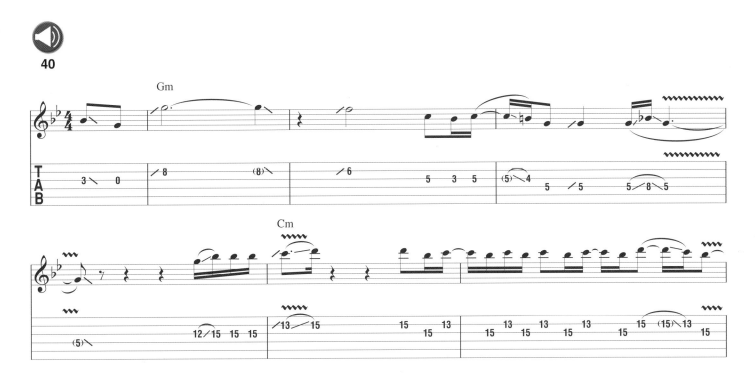

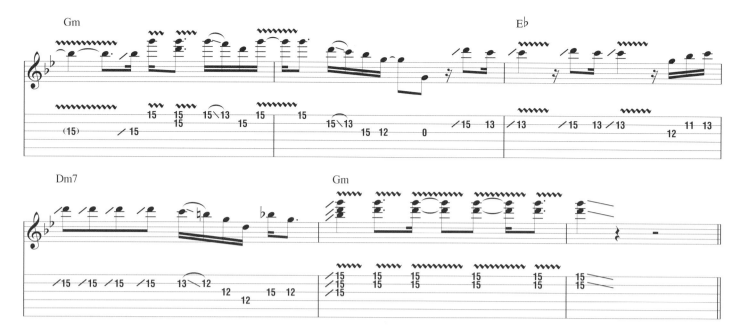

Against these non-blues changes (G–F–Em–D–C–Cm–G–D–G), I use a more melodic concept as opposed to a blues concept—I play inside the chords, grabbing various chord tones. In keeping with the mellow feel of this example, I use mostly notes from the top three strings, rather than finding those same notes on the thicker sounding lower strings.

41

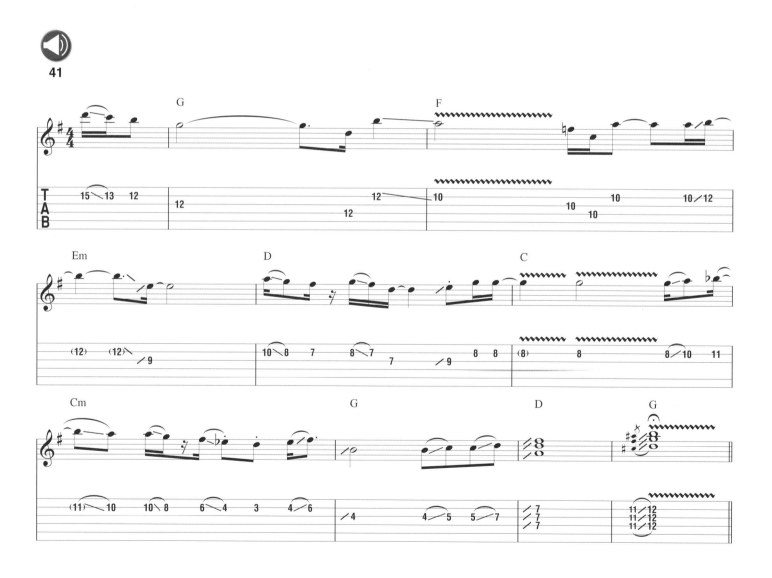

This is a different example of melodic slide guitar, kind of à la George Harrison, and played over a different type of change with a chord built on the ♭7th (G) instead of the major 7th (G♯). I play, once again, inside the chord changes. In progressions like these, it's very important to play melodically and not just play blues riffs.

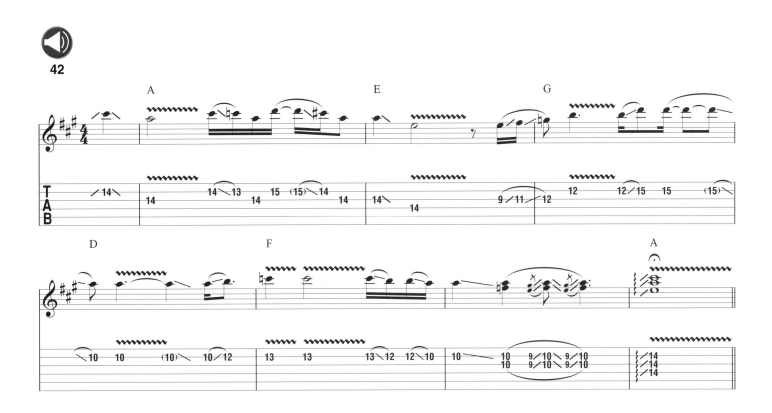

This solo is an extended example of how to play in a jazzy mode: somewhat outside the chord changes, less bluesy, often in minor, and with a lot of harmonic licks. Again, this illustrates how important it is to be able to think in standard tuning (where you can instantly play what pops into your head) as opposed to thinking in an open tuning (where you constantly have to transpose in your head).

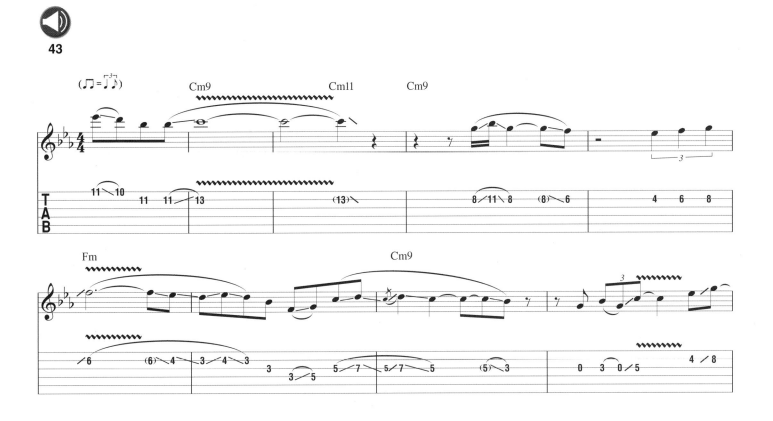

CHAPTER 6

ACOUSTIC SLIDE

There are significant differences in touch and approach between playing acoustic and electric slide guitar. First and foremost, you have much less sustain on an acoustic, so you have to rework your phrasing accordingly. And, unless your guitar has very high action, you hear more noise as the slide bangs against the neck—you have to work extra hard at dampening and keeping a light touch. On an acoustic, you should also use open strings as often as possible—the ringy, sustained sound they create is very characteristic of acoustic slide playing.

Although I do sometimes use open tunings for acoustic, I play the following examples in standard tuning (on a 1936 National that belongs to Derek Trucks, and used to belong to Bukka White.) All of the same advantages that you have playing slide in standard tuning on an electric apply to acoustic as well.

Here are some examples to get you going.

This is a melodic Delta blues lick in standard tuning that emulates open G, which is one of the more melodic open tunings (compared to, for instance, open E, which is darker and a more bluesy). I use the triad that standard tuning and open G have in common (G on the 12th fret of the 2nd, 3rd, and 4th strings), and that helps to imitate the open G sound.

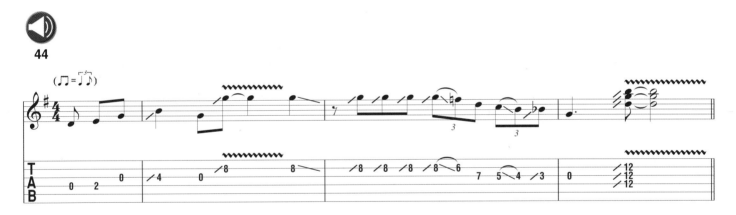

This open E-type acoustic lick shows how you can get the sounds of different open tunings within standard tuning. The dyad that begins this lick has an open E sound because the top two strings of the guitar are tuned to the same pitches in both open E and standard tuning.

This is a kind of a Son House/Delta blues riff that emulates open G and utilizes single strings as well.

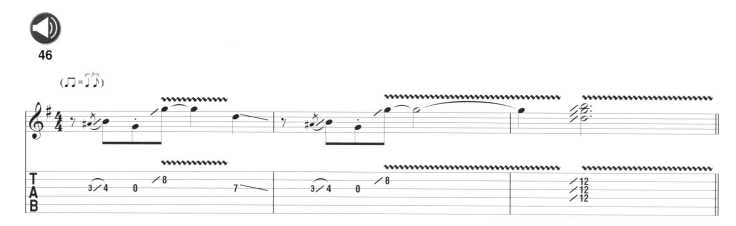

One of the advantages of open tuning is that, because your guitar is tuned to a chord, you can easily grab bass notes on lower strings to go along with a melody you're playing on higher strings. This is much trickier in standard tuning, but it can be done to a certain extent. In this example, I play one string at a time while letting the low E string ring on as a drone without touching it with the slide—this is very church-like.

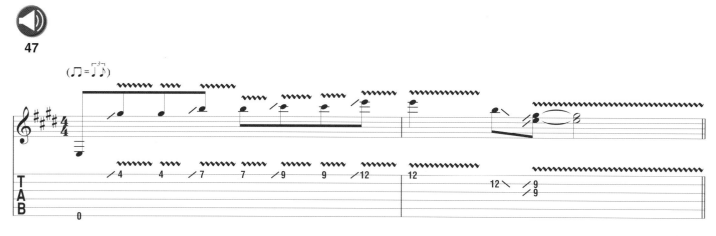

Here, I play over a G–C progression, illustrating a melodic slide sound. To achieve this mellow feel, I use notes from a G major scale, as opposed to taking the more pentatonic approach of blues playing.

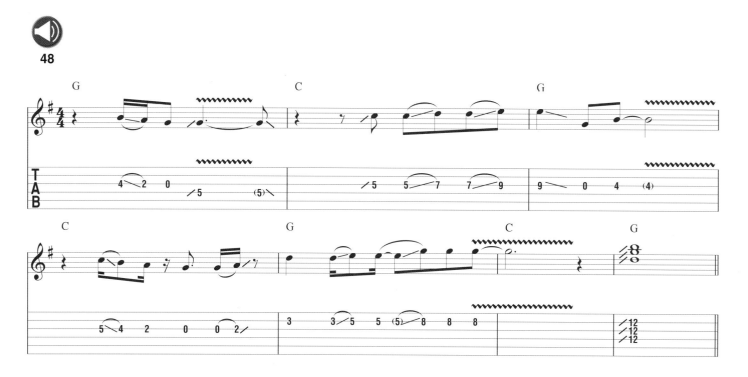

This blues solo features a wide range of acoustic slide licks. From licks using open strings (from the beginning through measure 2), to heavily vibratoed Delta licks (measures 19, 22–23, and 27–28), to electric-style riffs (measures 17–18), there's a lot of variety here. There are also wide ranges of dynamics and intensity, as there should be in any solo—but especially a long one.

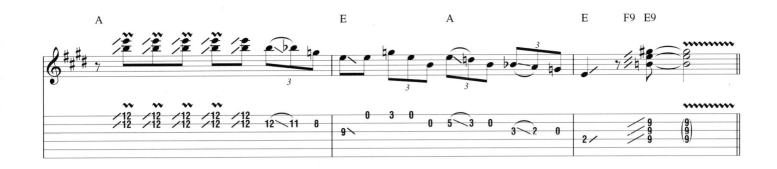

AFTERWORD

I hope you've enjoyed this book and that you've gotten a lot from it. Remember that mastering slide guitar is no different than learning any other instrumental technique—it takes a lot of practice. In particular, I can't stress enough how important it is to master right-hand dampening techniques—they're the key to my style of slide. So be patient, put your heart into it, and you'll get there.

Thanks for purchasing this book, and keep on playing!

A SELECTED WARREN HAYNES DISCOGRAPHY

WITH GOV'T MULE

Gov't Mule
Relativity, 1995

Live at Roseland Ballroom
Foundation Records, 1996

Dose
Capricorn Records, 1998

Live . . . With a Little Help from Our Friends
Capricorn Records, 1999

Life Before Insanity
Capricorn Records, 2000

The Deep End, Volume 1
ATO Records, 2001

The Deep End, Volume 2
ATO Records, 2002

WITH THE ALLMAN BROTHERS BAND

Seven Turns
Sony, 1990

Shades of Two Worlds
Sony, 1991

An Evening with the Allman Brothers Band: First Set
Sony, 1992

Where It All Begins
Sony, 1994

An Evening with the Allman Brothers Band: 2nd Set
Sony, 1995

Mycology: An Anthology
Sony, 1998

Hittin' the Note
Sanctuary Records, 2003

SOLO

Tales of Ordinary Madness
Megaforce, 1996

The Lone EP
ATO, 2003

APPENDIX

BACKING TRACKS FOR PRACTICING AND JAMMING

Here are the charts for the backing tracks to the five full-length, electric slide solos. You can jam along with these tracks and practice the slide techniques you've learned from this book.

BLUES SHUFFLE SOLO

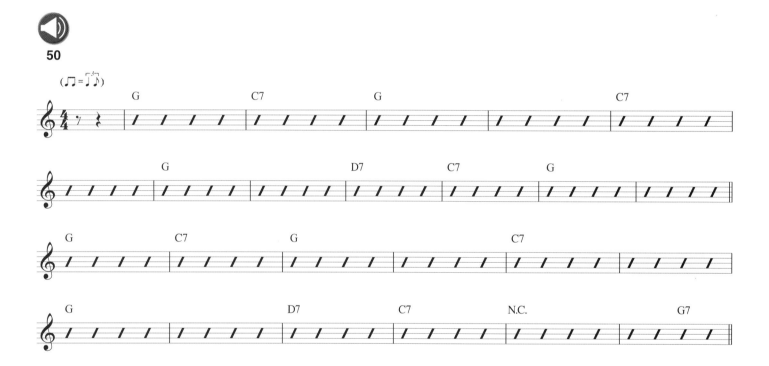

SLOW SOLO

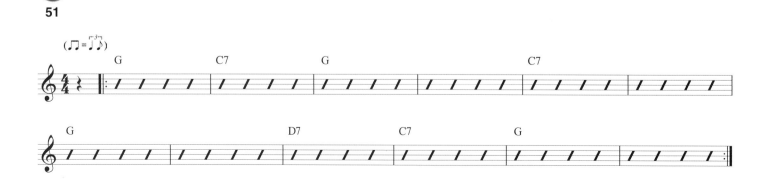

ADVANCED SOLO

52

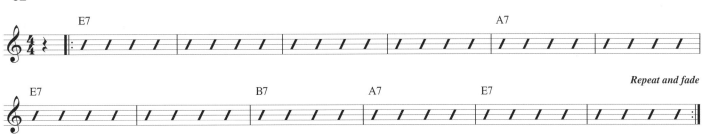

MINOR SOLO

53

EXTENDED JAZZY SOLO

54

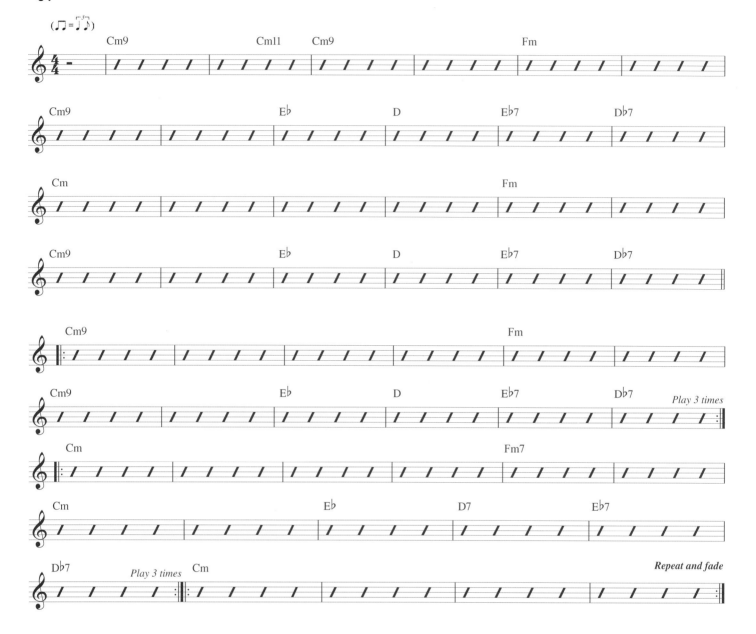

The Hottest Tab Songbooks Available For Guitar & Bass

PLAY IT LIKE IT IS **GUITAR** WITH TABLATURE — NOTE-FOR-NOTE TRANSCRIPTIONS

PLAY IT LIKE IT IS **BASS** WITH TABLATURE — NOTE-FOR-NOTE TRANSCRIPTIONS

Guitar Transcriptions

02501410	The Black Keys – Attack & Release	$19.99
02501629	The Black Keys – Brothers	$24.99
02501500	The Black Keys – A Collection	$22.99
02501766	The Black Keys – El Camino	$19.99
02501600	Black Label Society – Order of the Black	$22.99
02501510	Joe Bonamassa Collection	$24.99
00110278	Joe Bonamassa – Driving Towards the Daylight	$24.99
02501720	Joe Bonamassa – Dust Bowl	$29.99
00110294	Zac Brown Band – Uncaged	$22.99
02501565	Coheed and Cambria – Year of the Black Rainbow	$22.99
02506878	John Denver Anthology for Easy Guitar Revised Edition	$19.99
02506901	John Denver Authentic Guitar Style	$17.99
02506928	John Denver – Greatest Hits for Fingerstyle Guitar	$19.99
02500632	John Denver Collection Strum & Sing Series	$17.99
02501448	Best of Ronnie James Dio	$24.99
02500198	Best of Foreigner	$24.99
02501242	Guns N' Roses – Anthology	$29.99
02506953	Guns N' Roses – Appetite for Destruction	$24.99
02501286	Guns N' Roses Complete, Volume 1	$29.99
02501287	Guns N' Roses Complete, Volume 2	$29.99
02501755	Guns N' Roses – Greatest Hits	$29.99
02501193	Guns N' Roses – Use Your Illusion I	$27.99
02501194	Guns N' Roses – Use Your Illusion II	$24.99
02500458	Best of Warren Haynes	$29.99
02500476	Warren Haynes – Guide to Slide Guitar	$19.99
02501723	Warren Haynes – Man in Motion	$22.99
02500387	Best of Heart	$24.99
02500831	Jack Johnson – In Between Dreams	$22.99
02500653	Jack Johnson – On and On	$24.99
02500858	Jack Johnson – Strum & Sing	$19.99
02501564	Jack Johnson – To the Sea	$19.99

02500380	Lenny Kravitz – Greatest Hits	$22.99
02501093	Amos Lee	$19.95
02500129	Adrian Legg – Pickin' 'n' Squintin'	$19.95
02500362	Best of Little Feat	$22.99
02500305	Best of The Marshall Tucker Band	$24.99
02501077	Dave Matthews Band – Anthology	$22.99
02501502	John Mayer – Battle Studies	$22.99
02500986	John Mayer – Continuum	$24.99
02500705	John Mayer – Heavier Things	$24.99
02501513	John Mayer Live	$24.99
02500529	John Mayer – Room for Squares	$24.99
02506965	Metallica – ...And Justice for All	$24.99
02501626	Metallica – Classic Songs	$19.99
02501267	Metallica – Death Magnetic	$24.99
02506235	Metallica – 5 of the Best/Vol. 2	$12.95
02507018	Metallica – Kill 'Em All	$22.99
02501275	Metallica – Load	$29.99
02507920	Metallica – Master of Puppets	$24.99
02501195	Metallica – Metallica	$24.99
02501297	Metallica – ReLoad	$29.99
02507019	Metallica – Ride the Lightning	$24.99
02500279	Metallica – S&M Highlights	$27.99
02500846	Best of Steve Morse Band and Dixie Dregs	$19.95
02501324	Jason Mraz – We Sing, We Dance, We Steal Things.	$22.99
02500448	Best of Ted Nugent	$24.99
02500348	Ozzy Osbourne – Blizzard of Ozz	$22.99
02501277	Ozzy Osbourne – Diary of a Madman	$22.99
02507904	Ozzy Osbourne/Randy Rhoads Tribute	$24.99
02500680	Don't Stop Believin': The Steve Perry Anthology	$24.99
02500025	Primus Anthology – A-N (Guitar/Bass)	$22.99
02500091	Primus Anthology – O-Z (Guitar/Bass)	$27.99
02500468	Primus – Sailing the Seas of Cheese	$24.99
02500875	Queens of the Stone Age – Lullabies to Paralyze	$24.99
02501617	Joe Satriani – Black Swans and Wormhole Wizards	$24.99
02501299	Joe Satriani – Crystal Planet	$27.99

02501701	The Joe Satriani Collection	$24.99
02501205	Joe Satriani – The Extremist	$24.99
02500544	Joe Satriani – Strange Beautiful Music	$24.99
02500920	Joe Satriani – Super Colossal	$22.95
02506959	Joe Satriani – Surfing with the Alien	$22.99
02500188	Best of the Brian Setzer Orchestra	$22.99
02500985	Sex Pistols – Never Mind the Bollocks, Here's the Sex Pistols	$22.99
02500956	The Strokes – Is This It	$22.99
02501586	The Sword – Age of Winters	$19.99
02500799	Tenacious D	$22.99
02501035	Tenacious D – The Pick of Destiny	$19.99
02501263	Tesla – Time's Making Changes	$22.99
02501147	30 Easy Spanish Guitar Solos	$16.99
02500561	Learn Funk Guitar with Tower of Power's Jeff Tamelier	$22.99
02501440	Derek Trucks – Already Free	$24.99
02501007	Keith Urban – Love, Pain & The Whole Crazy Thing	$24.95
00102592	Jack White – Blunderbuss	$19.99
02500636	The White Stripes – Elephant	$24.99
02500583	The White Stripes – White Blood Cells	$22.99
02501092	Wilco – Sky Blue Sky	$24.99
02500431	Best of Johnny Winter	$24.99
02501716	Zakk Wylde Anthology	$24.99
02500700	Zakk Wylde – Legendary Licks	$19.95

Bass Transcriptions

02501108	Bass Virtuosos	$19.95
02500117	Black Sabbath – Riff by Riff Bass	$22.99
02506966	Guns N' Roses – Appetite for Destruction	$22.99
02501522	John Mayer Anthology for Bass, Vol. 1	$24.99
02500771	Best of Rancid for Bass	$24.99
02501120	Best of Tower of Power for Bass	$19.95
02500317	Victor Wooten Songbook	$24.99

See your local music dealer or contact:

Prices, contents, and availability subject to change without notice.

HAL•LEONARD® GUITAR PLAY-ALONG

INCLUDES TAB

AUDIO ACCESS INCLUDED

This series will help you play your favorite songs quickly and easily. Just follow the tab and listen to the audio to hear how the guitar should sound, and then play along using the separate backing tracks.

Playback tools are provided for slowing down the tempo without changing pitch and looping challenging parts. The melody and lyrics are included in the book so that you can sing or simply follow along.

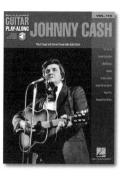

107. CREAM
00701069...................$17.99

108. THE WHO
00701053...................$17.99

109. STEVE MILLER
00701054...................$19.99

110. SLIDE GUITAR HITS
00701055...................$17.99

111. JOHN MELLENCAMP
00701056...................$14.99

112. QUEEN
00701052...................$16.99

113. JIM CROCE
00701058...................$19.99

114. BON JOVI
00701060...................$17.99

115. JOHNNY CASH
00701070...................$17.99

116. THE VENTURES
00701124...................$17.99

117. BRAD PAISLEY
00701224...................$16.99

118. ERIC JOHNSON
00701353...................$17.99

119. AC/DC CLASSICS
00701356...................$19.99

120. PROGRESSIVE ROCK
00701457...................$14.99

121. U2
00701508...................$17.99

122. CROSBY, STILLS & NASH
00701610...................$16.99

123. LENNON & McCARTNEY ACOUSTIC
00701614...................$16.99

124. SMOOTH JAZZ
00200664...................$16.99

125. JEFF BECK
00701687...................$19.99

126. BOB MARLEY
00701701...................$17.99

127. 1970S ROCK
00701739...................$17.99

128. 1960S ROCK
00701740...................$14.99

129. MEGADETH
00701741...................$17.99

130. IRON MAIDEN
00701742...................$17.99

131. 1990S ROCK
00701743...................$14.99

132. COUNTRY ROCK
00701757...................$15.99

133. TAYLOR SWIFT
00701894...................$16.99

135. MINOR BLUES
00151350...................$17.99

136. GUITAR THEMES
00701922...................$14.99

137. IRISH TUNES
00701966...................$15.99

138. BLUEGRASS CLASSICS
00701967...................$17.99

139. GARY MOORE
00702370...................$17.99

140. MORE STEVIE RAY VAUGHAN
00702396...................$19.99

141. ACOUSTIC HITS
00702401...................$16.99

142. GEORGE HARRISON
00237697...................$17.99

143. SLASH
00702425...................$19.99

144. DJANGO REINHARDT
00702531...................$17.99

145. DEF LEPPARD
00702532...................$19.99

146. ROBERT JOHNSON
00702533...................$16.99

147. SIMON & GARFUNKEL
14041591...................$17.99

148. BOB DYLAN
14041592...................$17.99

149. AC/DC HITS
14041593...................$19.99

150. ZAKK WYLDE
02501717...................$19.99

151. J.S. BACH
02501730...................$16.99

152. JOE BONAMASSA
02501751...................$24.99

153. RED HOT CHILI PEPPERS
00702990...................$22.99

155. ERIC CLAPTON – FROM THE ALBUM UNPLUGGED
00703085...................$17.99

156. SLAYER
00703770...................$19.99

157. FLEETWOOD MAC
00101382...................$17.99

159. WES MONTGOMERY
00102593...................$22.99

160. T-BONE WALKER
00102641...................$17.99

161. THE EAGLES – ACOUSTIC
00102659...................$19.99

162. THE EAGLES HITS
00102667...................$17.99

163. PANTERA
00103036...................$19.99

164. VAN HALEN 1986-1995
00110270...................$19.99

165. GREEN DAY
00210343...................$17.99

166. MODERN BLUES
00700764...................$16.99

167. DREAM THEATER
00111938...................$24.99

168. KISS
00113421...................$17.99

169. TAYLOR SWIFT
00115982...................$16.99

170. THREE DAYS GRACE
00117337...................$16.99

171. JAMES BROWN
00117420...................$16.99

172. THE DOOBIE BROTHERS
00119670...................$17.99

173. TRANS-SIBERIAN ORCHESTRA
00119907...................$19.99

174. SCORPIONS
00122119...................$19.99

175. MICHAEL SCHENKER
00122127...................$17.99

176. BLUES BREAKERS WITH JOHN MAYALL & ERIC CLAPTON
00122132...................$19.99

177. ALBERT KING
00123271...................$17.99

178. JASON MRAZ
00124165...................$17.99

179. RAMONES
00127073...................$16.99

180. BRUNO MARS
00129706...................$16.99

181. JACK JOHNSON
00129854...................$16.99

182. SOUNDGARDEN
00138161...................$17.99

183. BUDDY GUY
00138240...................$17.99

184. KENNY WAYNE SHEPHERD
00138258...................$17.99

185. JOE SATRIANI
00139457...................$19.99

186. GRATEFUL DEAD
00139459...................$17.99

187. JOHN DENVER
00140839...................$19.99

188. MÖTLEY CRUE
00141145...................$19.99

189. JOHN MAYER
00144350...................$19.99

190. DEEP PURPLE
00146152...................$19.99

191. PINK FLOYD CLASSICS
00146164...................$17.99

192. JUDAS PRIEST
00151352...................$19.99

193. STEVE VAI
00156028...................$19.99

194. PEARL JAM
00157925...................$17.99

195. METALLICA: 1983-1988
00234291...................$22.99

196. METALLICA: 1991-2016
00234292...................$19.99

HAL•LEONARD®

For complete songlists, visit
Hal Leonard online at
www.halleonard.com

Prices, contents, and availability subject to
change without notice.

GUITAR *signature licks*

Signature Licks book/audio packs provide a step-by-step breakdown of "right from the record" riffs, licks, and solos so you can jam along with your favorite bands. They contain performance notes and an overview of each artist's or group's style, with note-for-note transcriptions in notes and tab. The online audio tracks feature full-band demos at both normal and slow speeds.

AC/DC
14041352.................$24.99

AEROSMITH 1973-1979
00695106.................$24.99

AEROSMITH 1979-1998
00695219................. $22.95

DUANE ALLMAN
00696042.................$22.99

BEST OF CHET ATKINS
00695752.................$24.99

AVENGED SEVENFOLD
00696473.................$24.99

THE BEATLES
00298845.................$24.99

BEST OF THE BEATLES FOR ACOUSTIC GUITAR
00695453.................$24.99

THE BEATLES HITS
00695049.................$24.95

JEFF BECK
00696427.................$24.99

BEST OF GEORGE BENSON
00695418.................$22.99

BEST OF BLACK SABBATH
00695249.................$24.99

BLUES BREAKERS WITH JOHN MAYALL & ERIC CLAPTON
00696374.................$24.99

BON JOVI
00696380.................$22.99

ROY BUCHANAN
00696654.................$22.99

KENNY BURRELL
00695830.................$27.99

BEST OF CHARLIE CHRISTIAN
00695584.................$24.99

BEST OF ERIC CLAPTON
00695038.................$24.99

ERIC CLAPTON – FROM THE ALBUM UNPLUGGED
00695250.................$24.99

BEST OF CREAM
00695251.................$24.99

THE DOORS
00695373................. $22.95

DEEP PURPLE – GREATEST HITS
00695625.................$24.99

DREAM THEATER
00111943.................$24.99

TOMMY EMMANUEL
00696409................. $22.99

ESSENTIAL JAZZ GUITAR
00695875................. $19.99

FLEETWOOD MAC
00696416................. $22.99

ROBBEN FORD
00695903................. $22.95

BEST OF GRANT GREEN
00695747.................$24.99

PETER GREEN
00145386.................$24.99

BEST OF GUNS N' ROSES
00695183.................$24.99

THE BEST OF BUDDY GUY
00695186................. $22.99

JIM HALL
00695848 ....$29.99

JIMI HENDRIX
00696560.................$24.99

JIMI HENDRIX – VOLUME 2
00695835 ....$24.99

JOHN LEE HOOKER
00695894................. $22.99

BEST OF JAZZ GUITAR
00695586.................$29.99

ERIC JOHNSON
00699317.................$24.99

ROBERT JOHNSON
00695264.................$24.99

BARNEY KESSEL
00696009.................$24.99

THE ESSENTIAL ALBERT KING
00695713.................$24.99

B.B. KING – BLUES LEGEND
00696039................. $22.99

B.B. KING – THE DEFINITIVE COLLECTION
00695635.................$22.99

MARK KNOPFLER
00695178.................$24.99

LYNYRD SKYNYRD
00695872.................$24.99

THE BEST OF YNGWIE MALMSTEEN
00695669.................$24.99

BEST OF PAT MARTINO
00695632.................$24.99

MEGADETH
00696421.................$22.99

WES MONTGOMERY
00695387.................$24.99

BEST OF NIRVANA
00695483.................$24.95

VERY BEST OF OZZY OSBOURNE
00695431.................$22.99

BRAD PAISLEY
00696379.................$22.99

BEST OF JOE PASS
00695730.................$24.99

TOM PETTY
00696021.................$24.99

PINK FLOYD
00103659.................$27.99

THE GUITARS OF ELVIS
00174800.................$22.99

BEST OF QUEEN
00695097.................$24.99

RADIOHEAD
00109304.................$24.99

BEST OF RAGE AGAINST THE MACHINE
00695480.................$24.99

JERRY REED
00118236 ....$22.99

BEST OF DJANGO REINHARDT
00695660.................$27.99

BEST OF ROCK 'N' ROLL GUITAR
00695559.................$24.99

BEST OF ROCKABILLY GUITAR
00695785.................$19.99

BEST OF CARLOS SANTANA
00174664.................$22.99

BEST OF JOE SATRIANI
00695216.................$24.99

SLASH
00696576.................$22.99

SLAYER
00121281.................$22.99

BEST OF SOUTHERN ROCK
00695560................. $19.95

STEELY DAN
00696015.................$22.99

MIKE STERN
00695800.................$27.99

BEST OF SURF GUITAR
00695822.................$22.99

STEVE VAI
00673247.................$24.99

STEVE VAI – ALIEN LOVE SECRETS: THE NAKED VAMPS
00695223.................$22.95

STEVE VAI – FIRE GARDEN: THE NAKED VAMPS
00695166.................$22.95

STEVE VAI – THE ULTRA ZONE: NAKED VAMPS
00695684.................$22.95

VAN HALEN
00110227.................$24.99

THE GUITAR STYLE OF STEVIE RAY VAUGHAN
00695155.................$24.95

BEST OF THE VENTURES
00695772.................$24.99

THE WHO – 2ND ED.
00695561.................$22.95

JOHNNY WINTER
00695951.................$24.99

YES
00113120.................$24.99

NEIL YOUNG – GREATEST HITS
00695988.................$24.99

BEST OF ZZ TOP
00695738.................$24.99

HAL•LEONARD®
www.halleonard.com

COMPLETE DESCRIPTIONS AND SONGLISTS ONLINE!
Prices, contents and availability subject to change without notice.